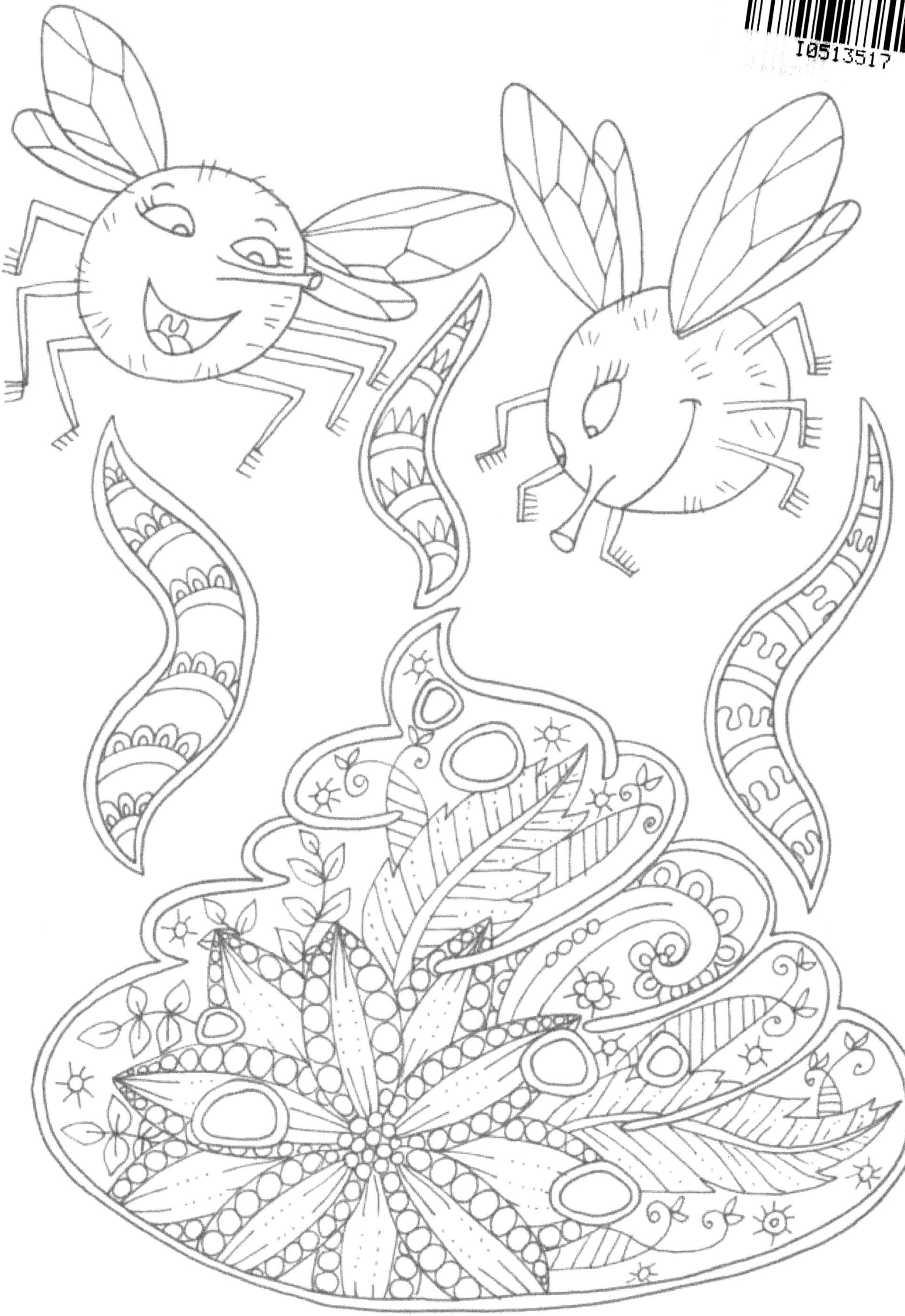

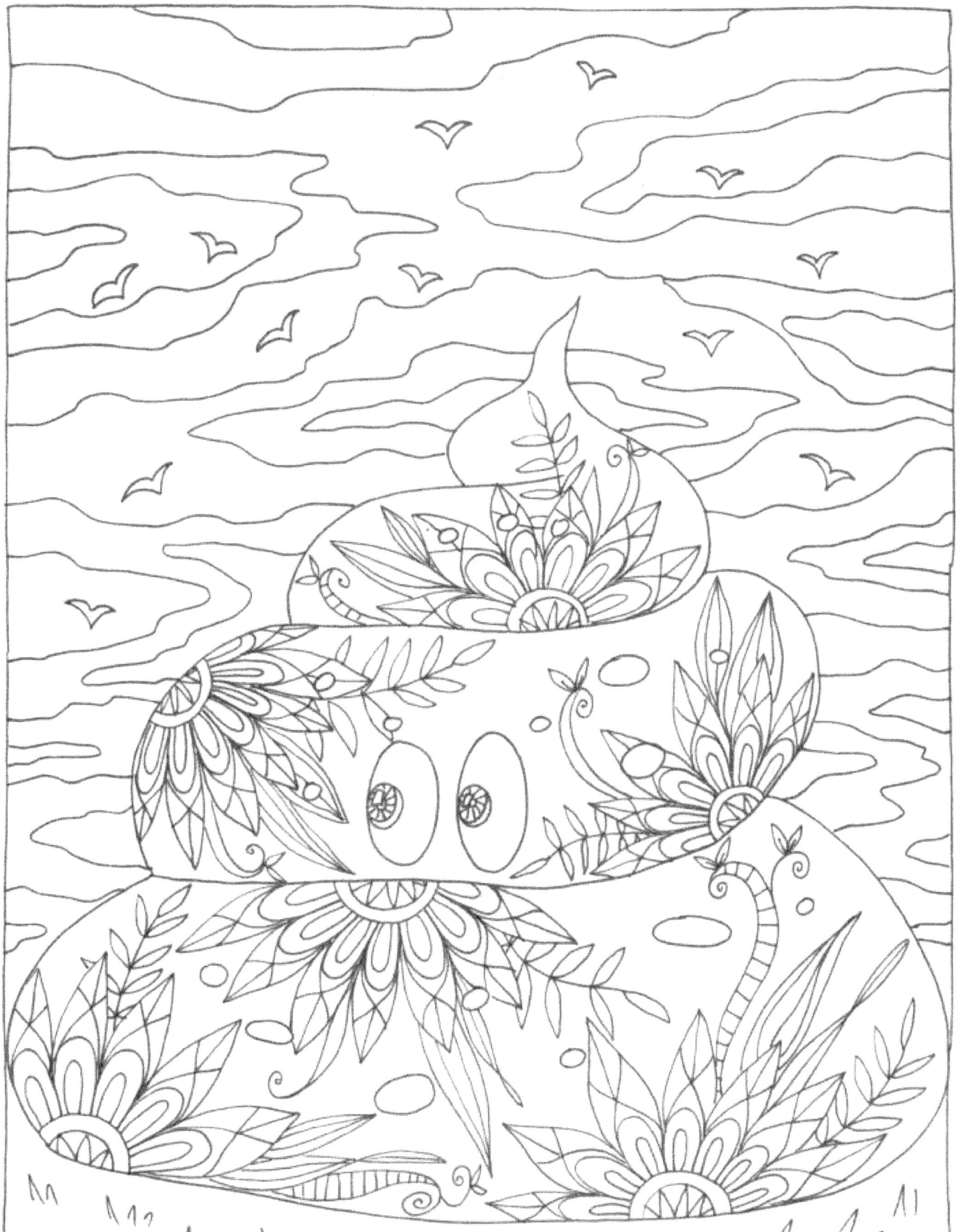

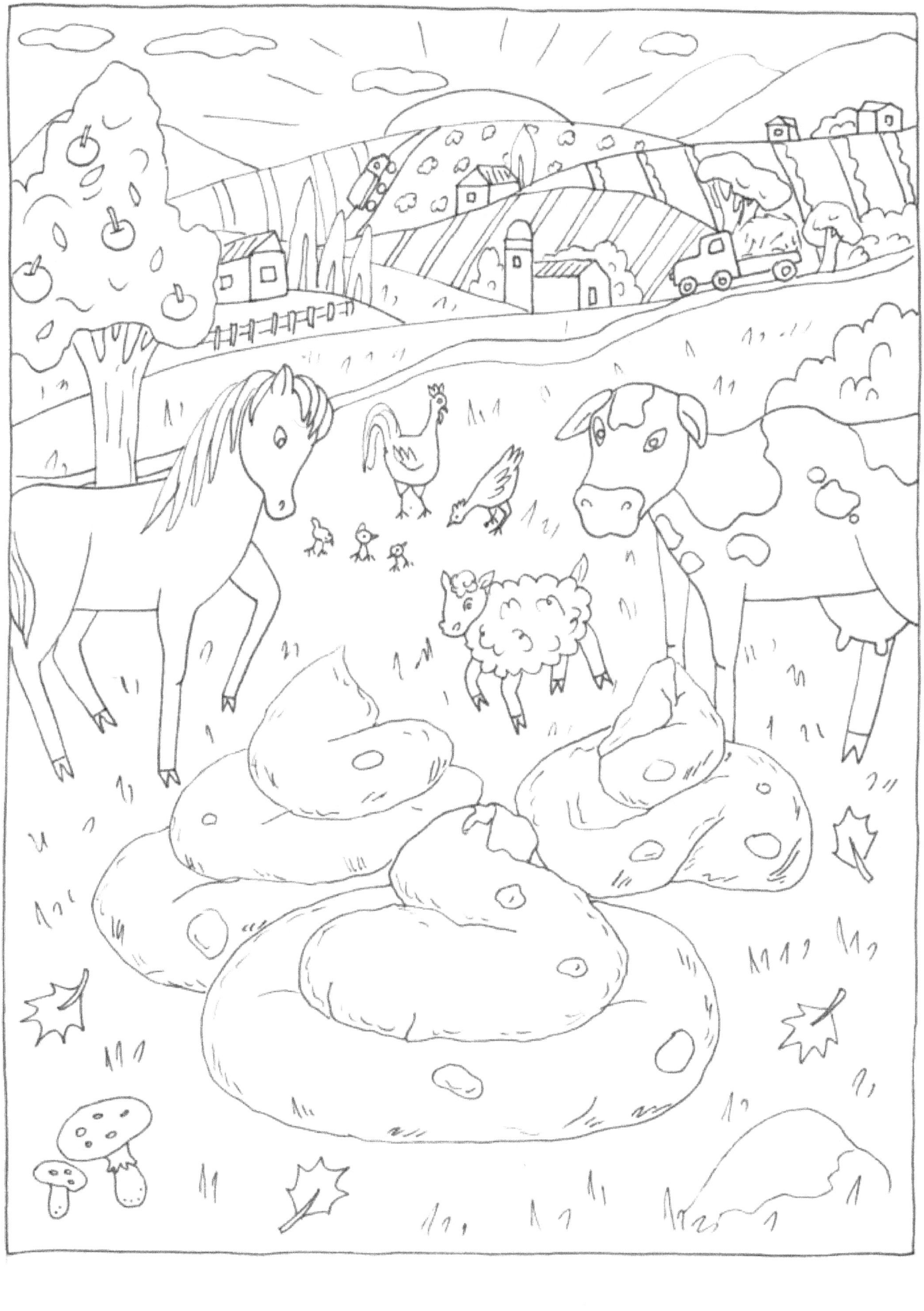

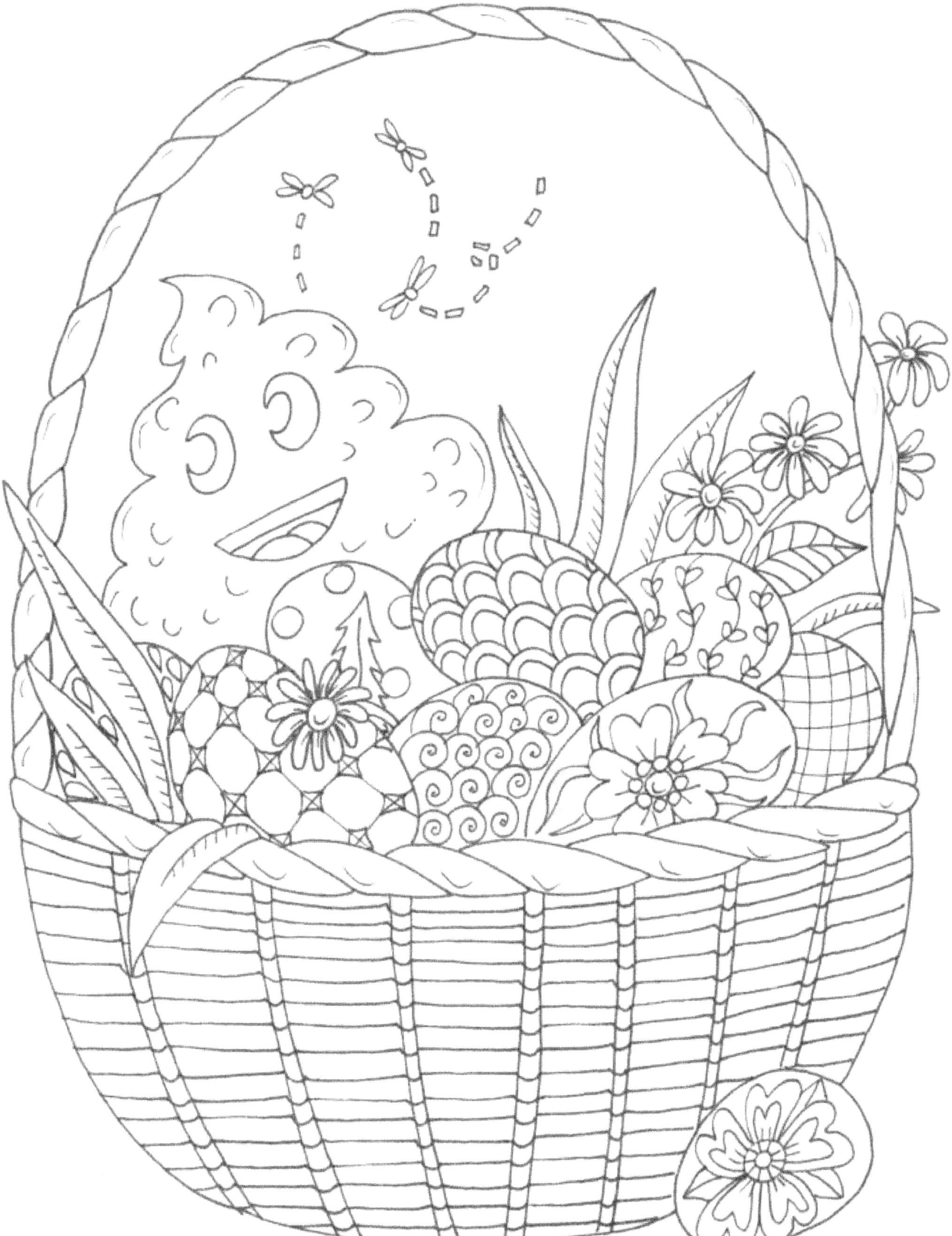

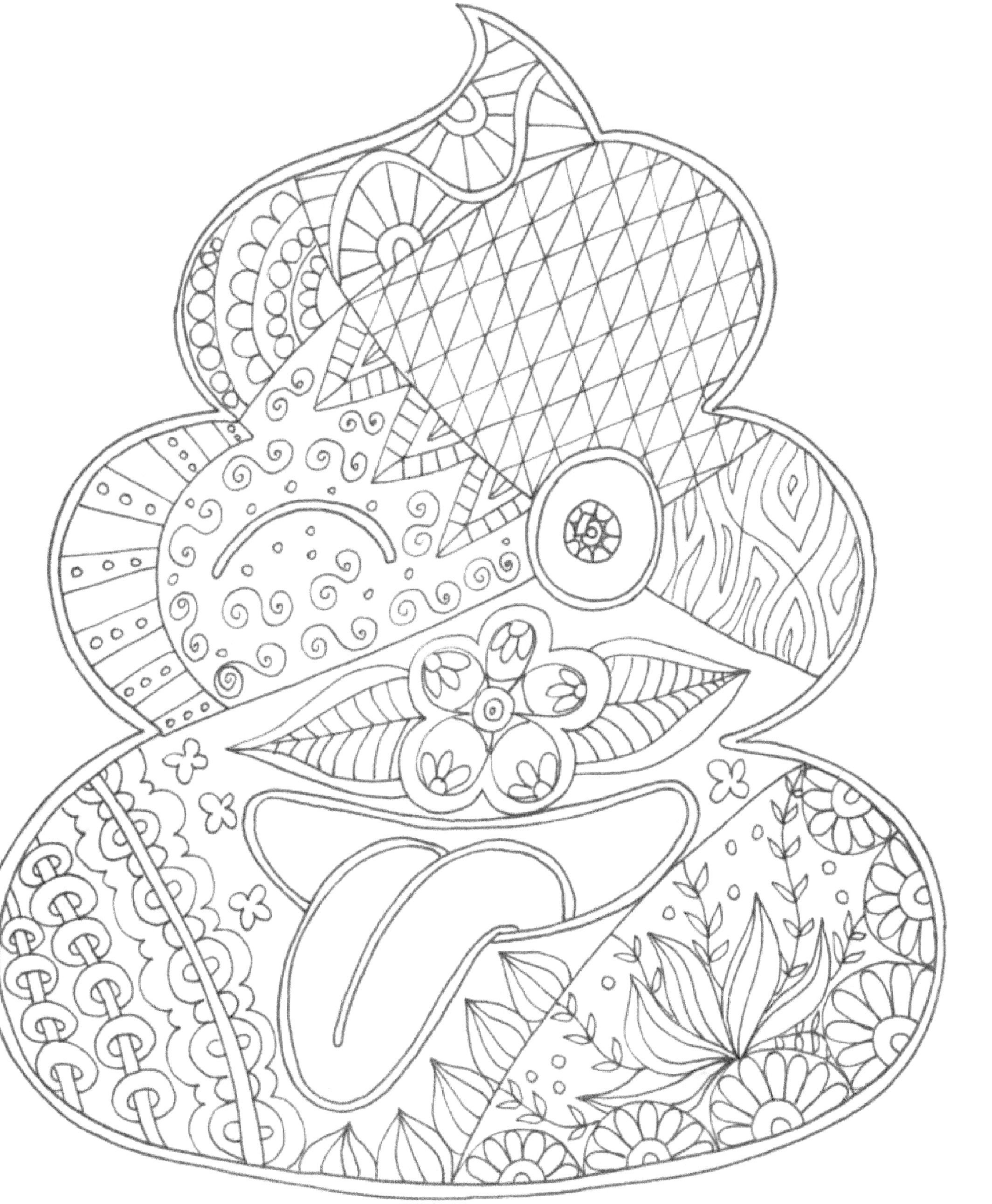

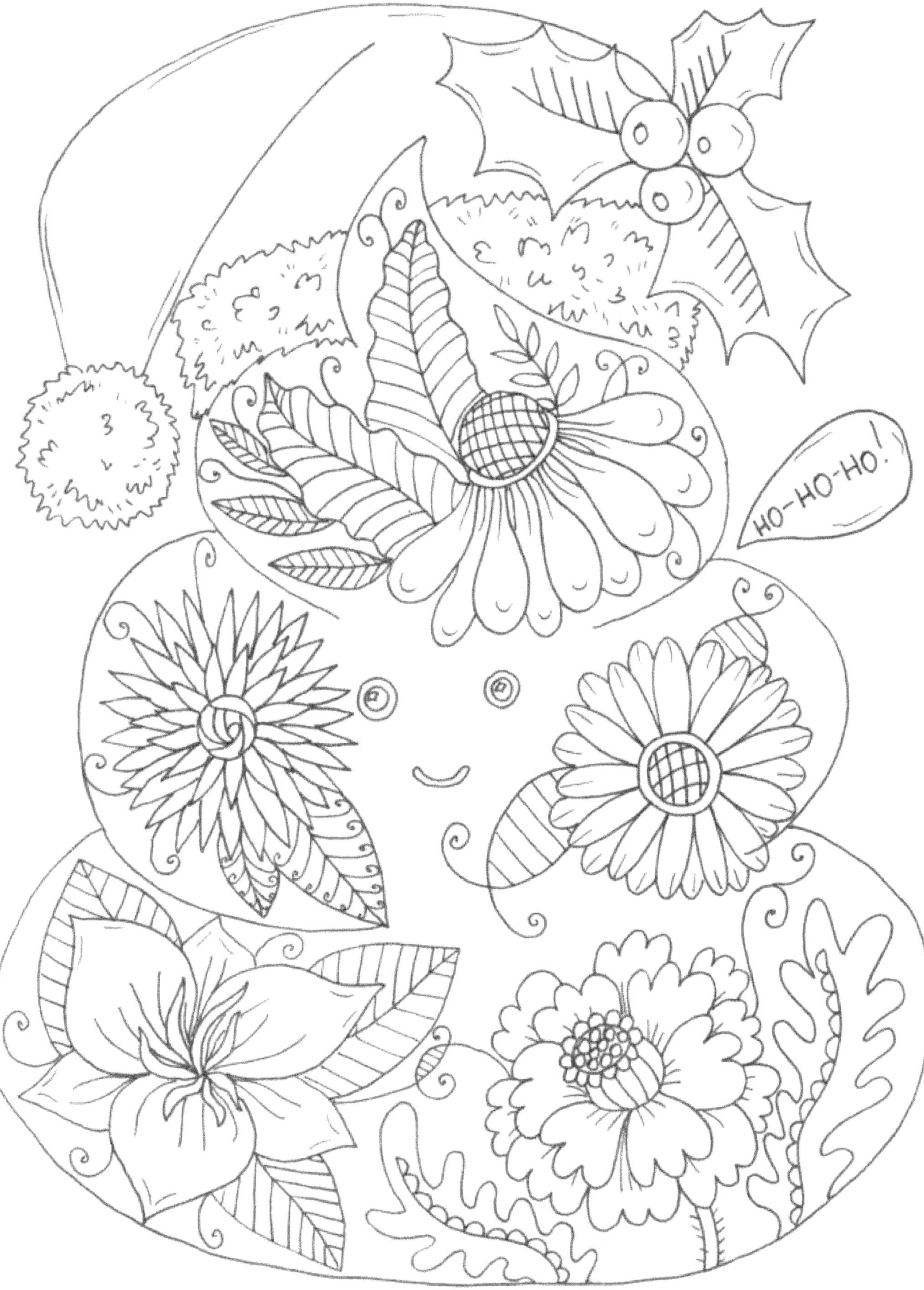
HO-HO-HO!

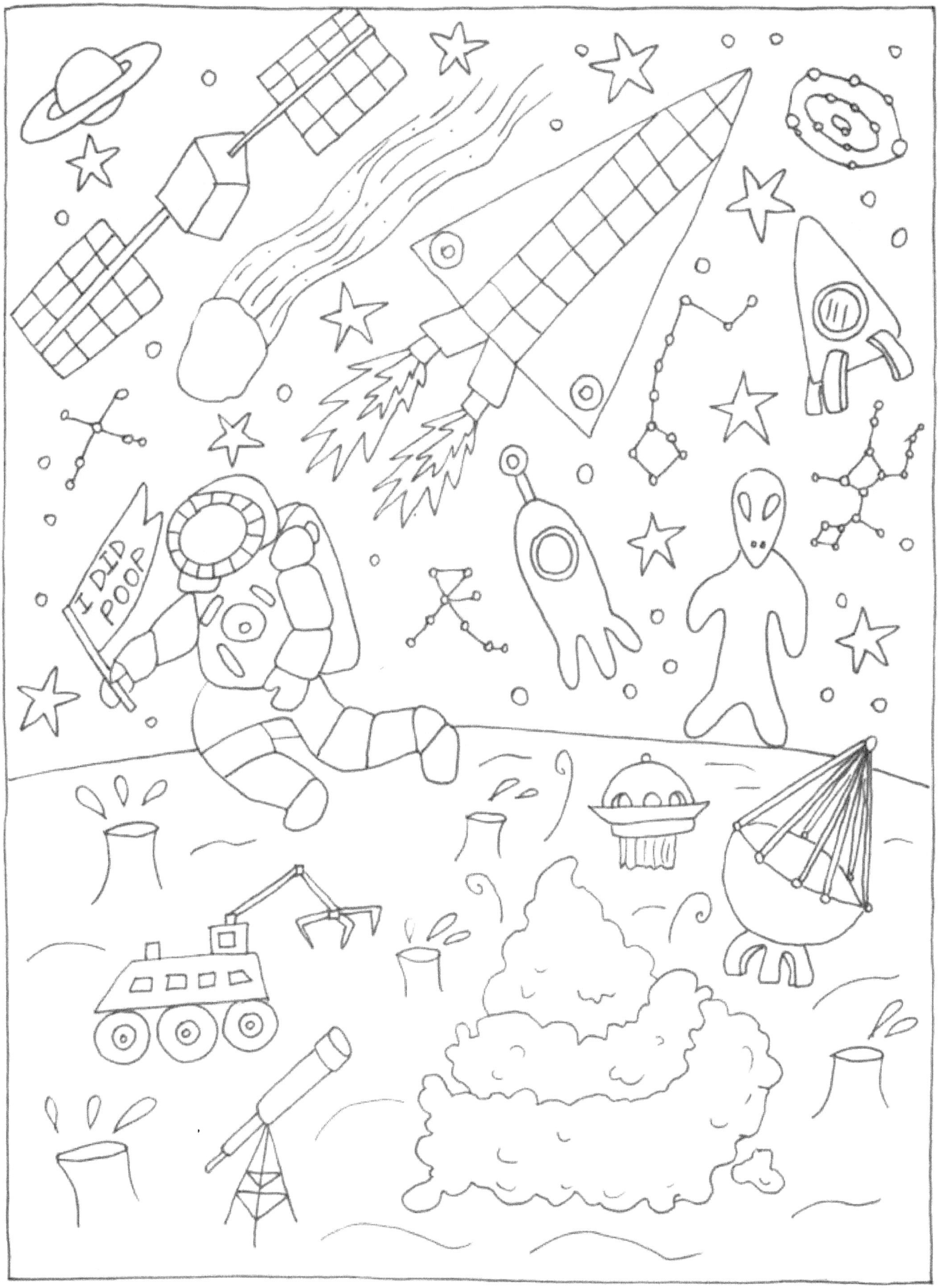
I DID POOP

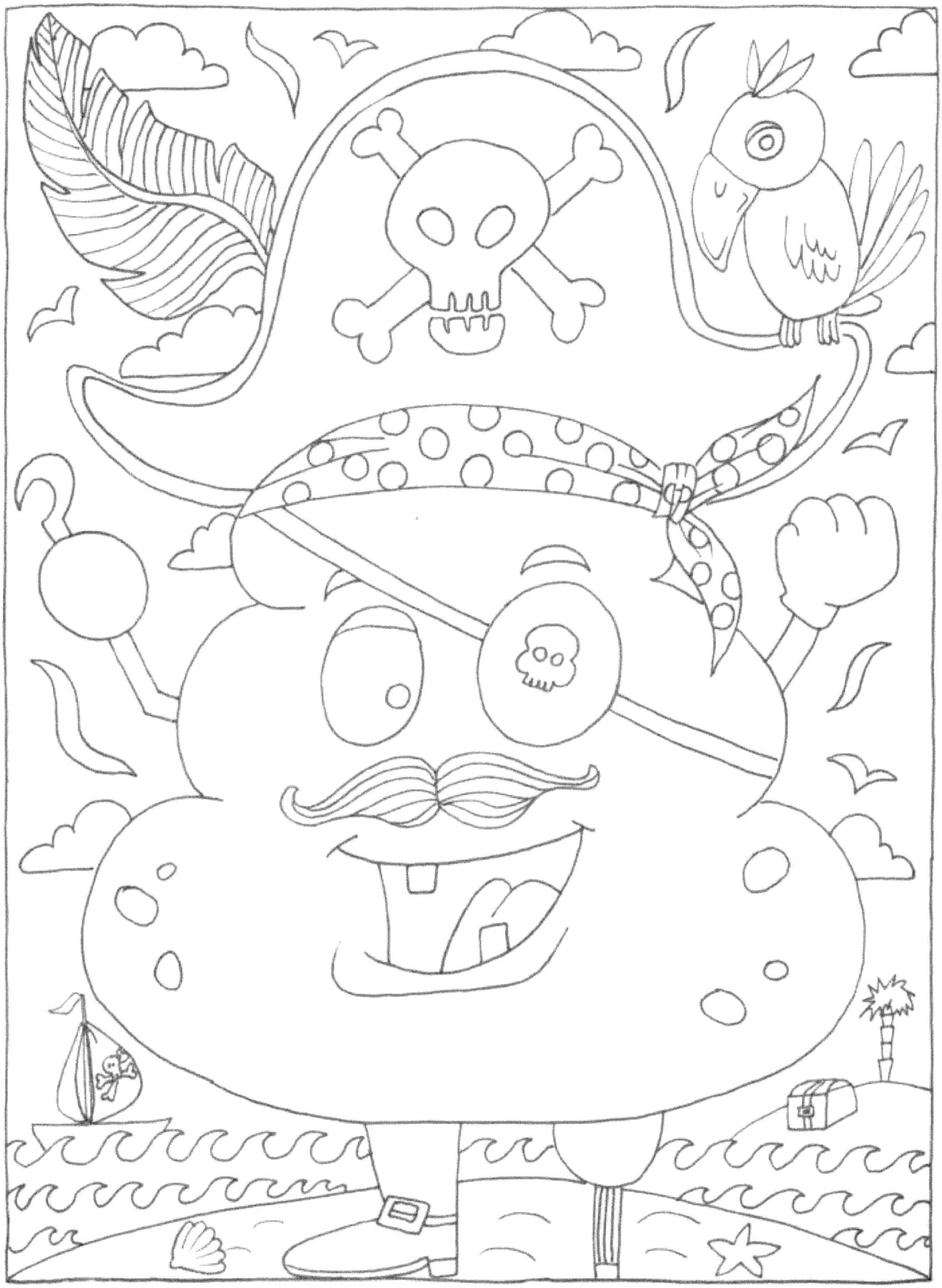

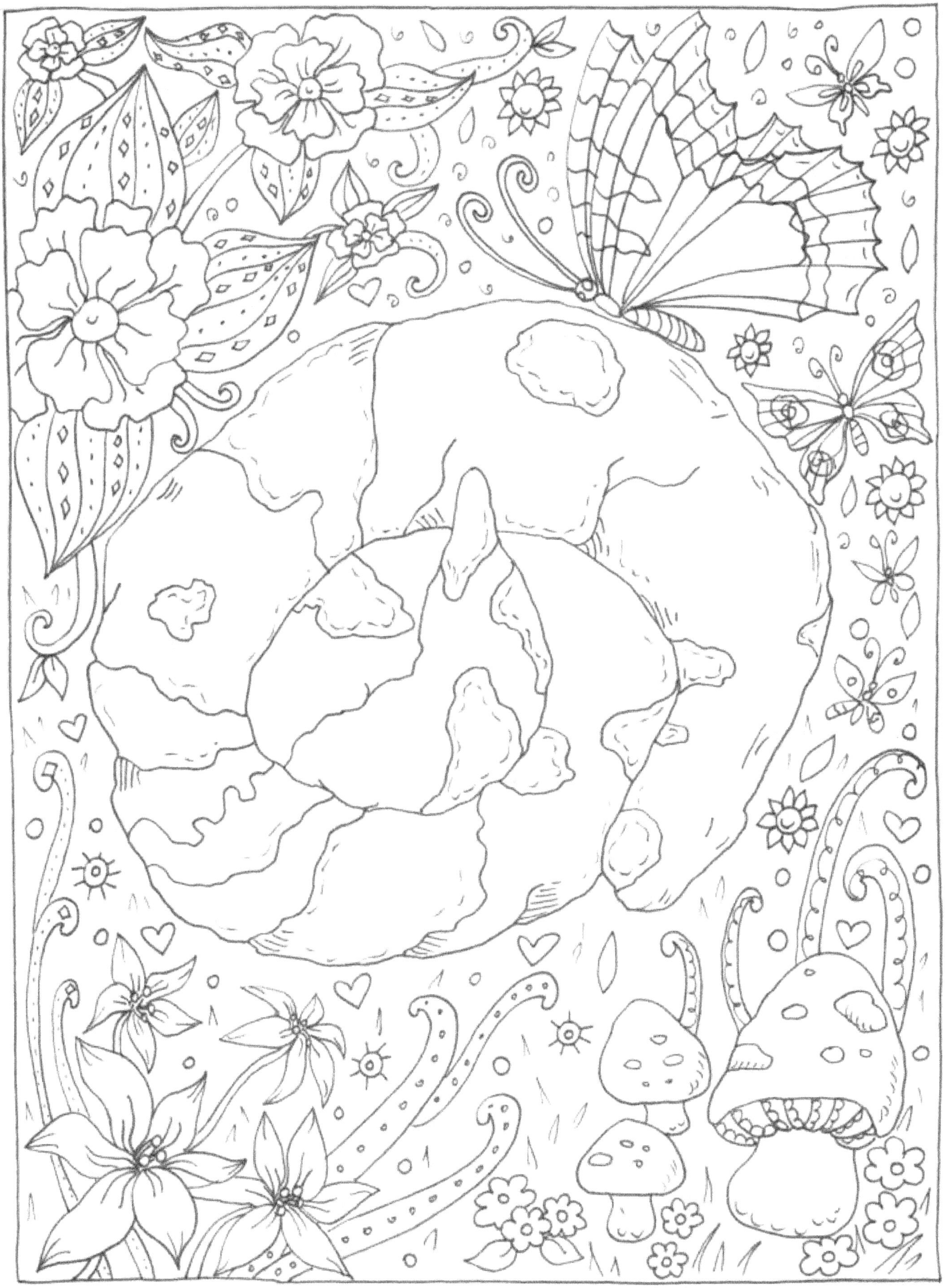

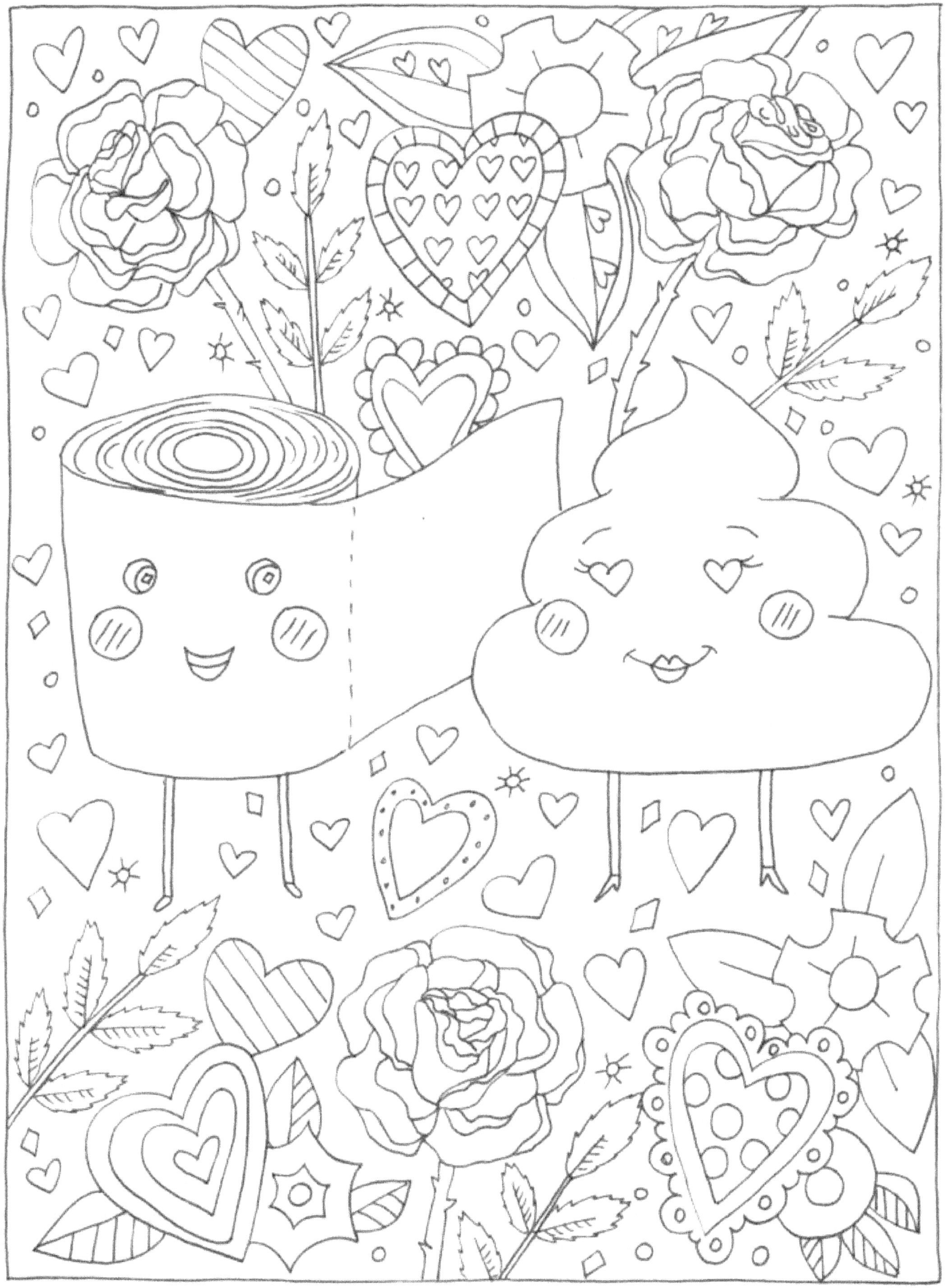

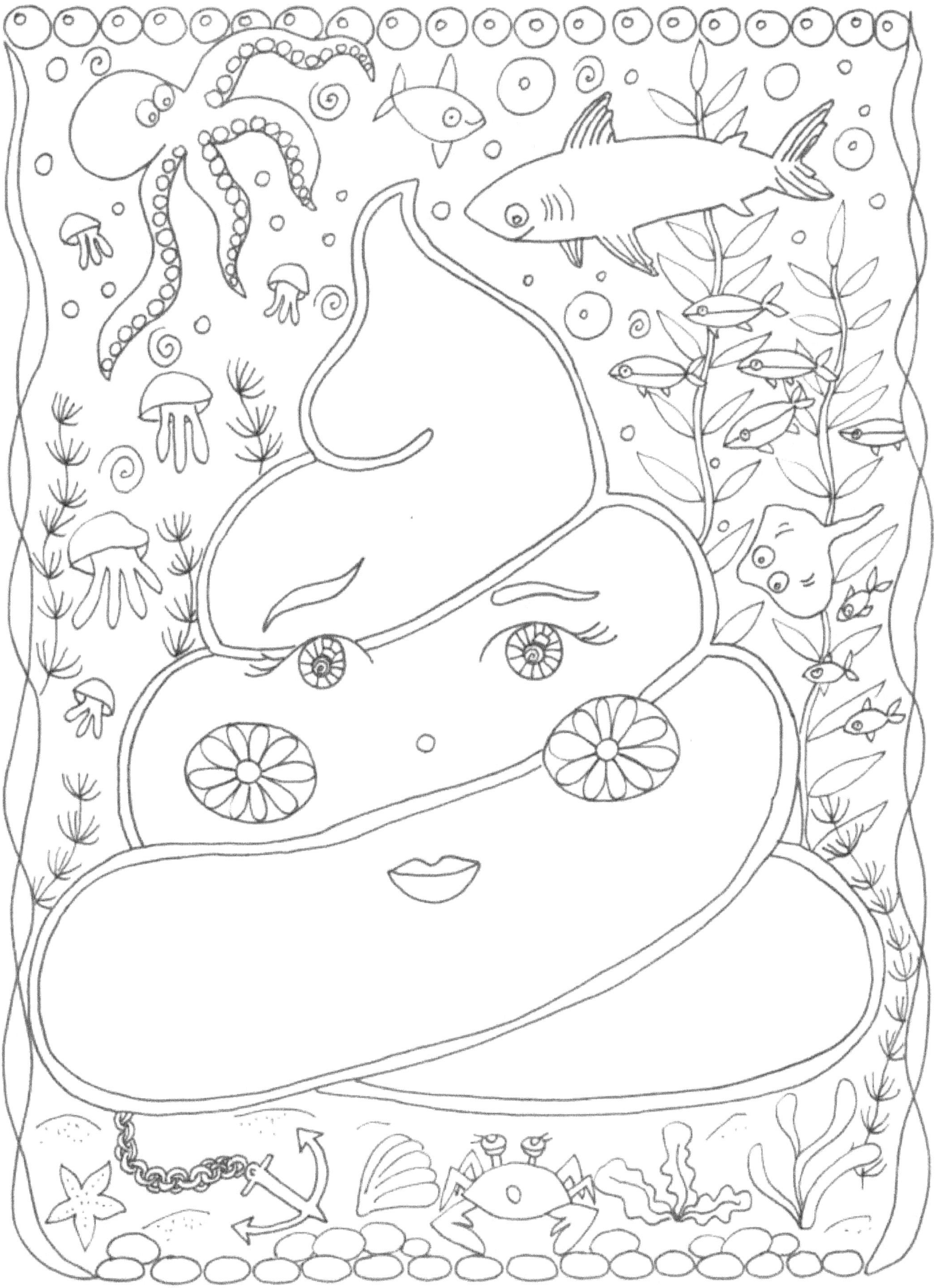

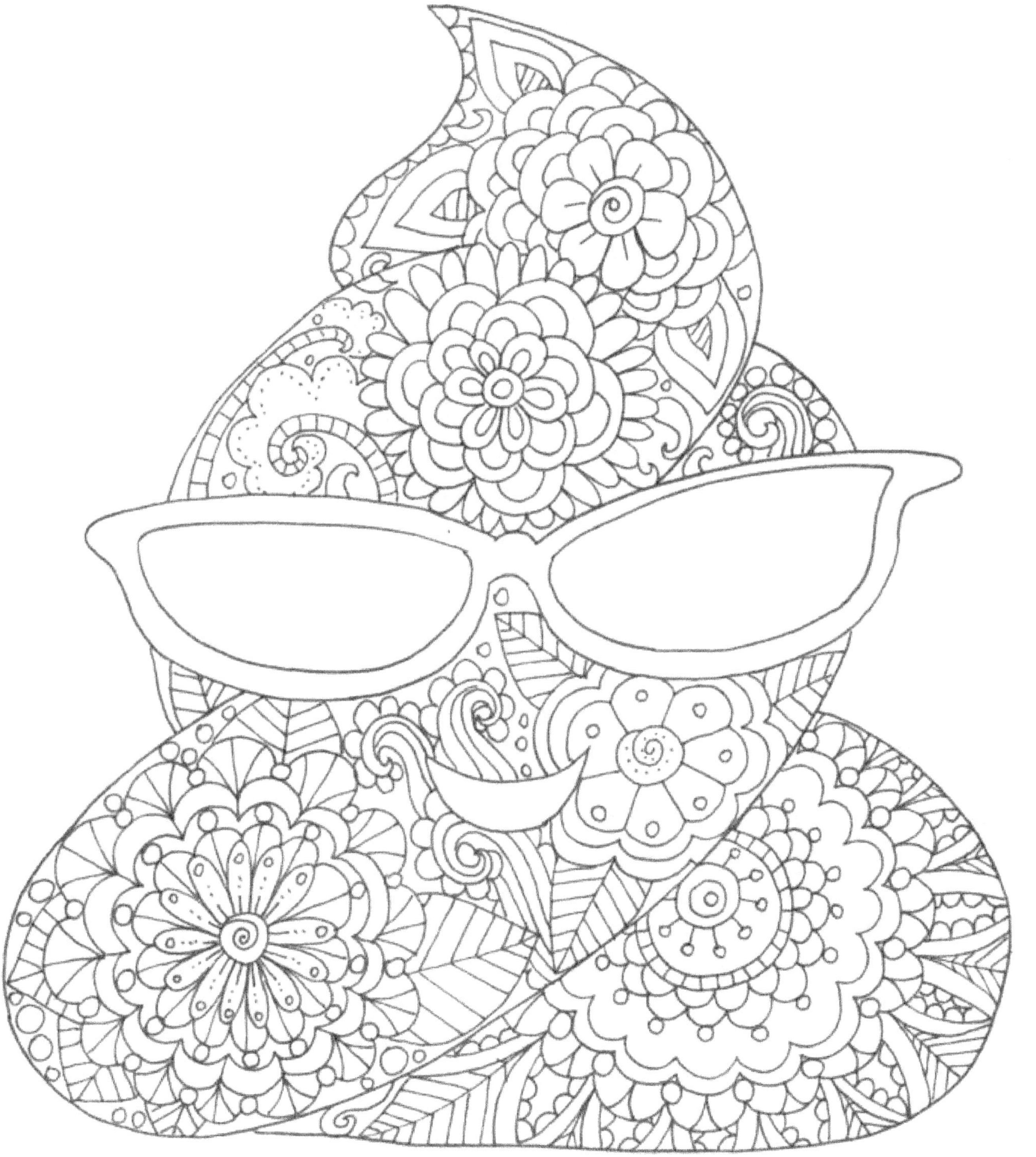

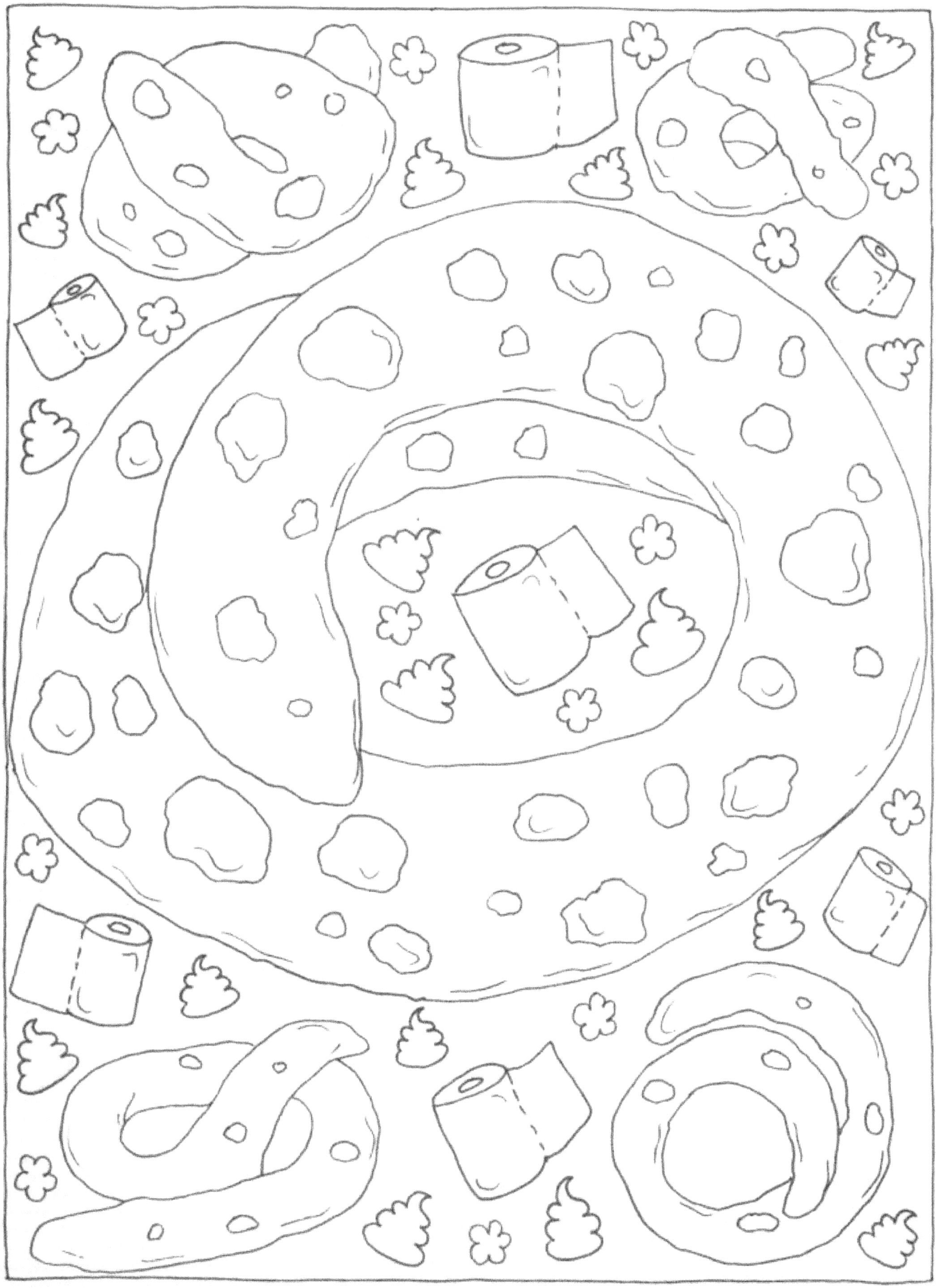

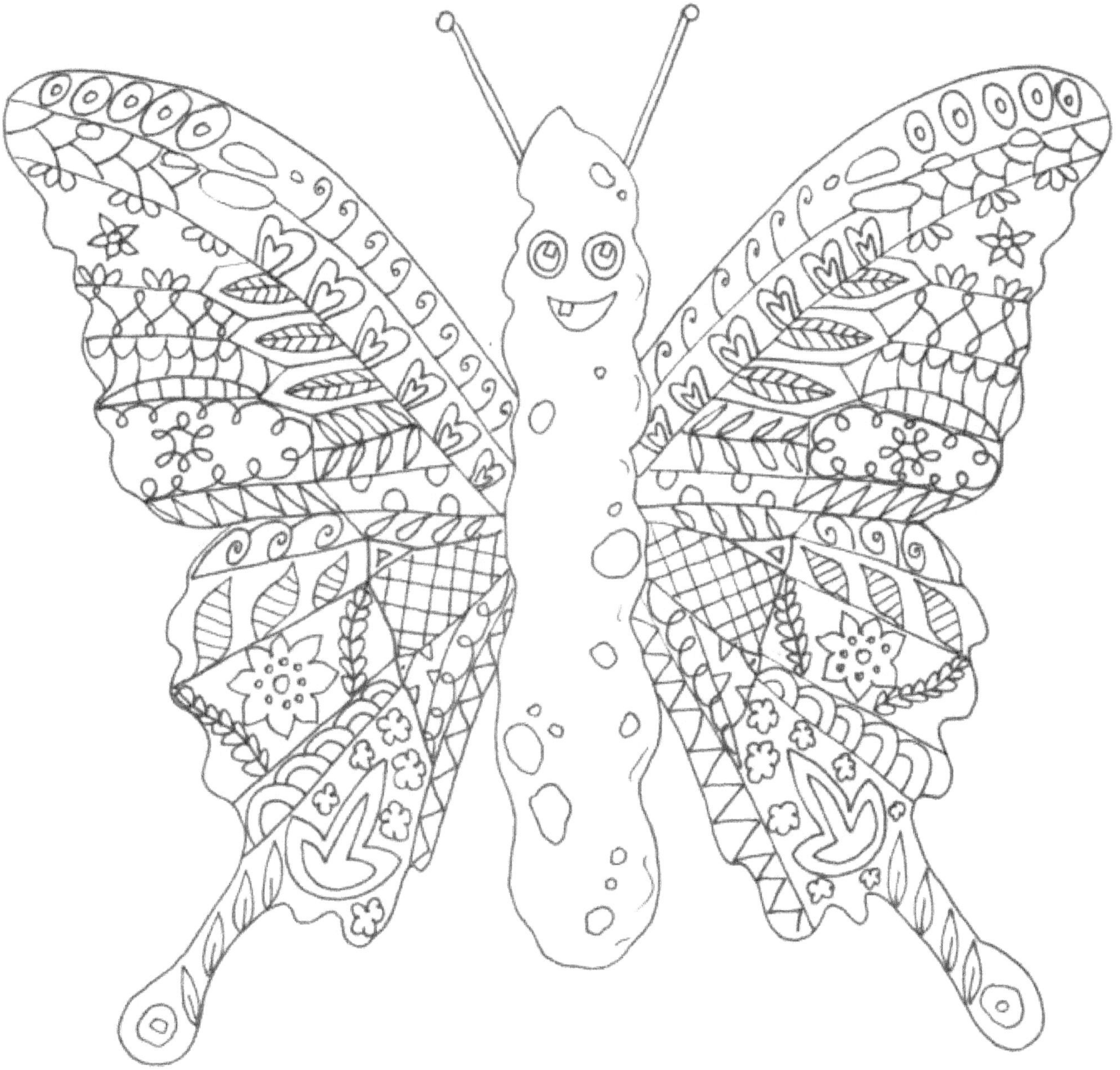

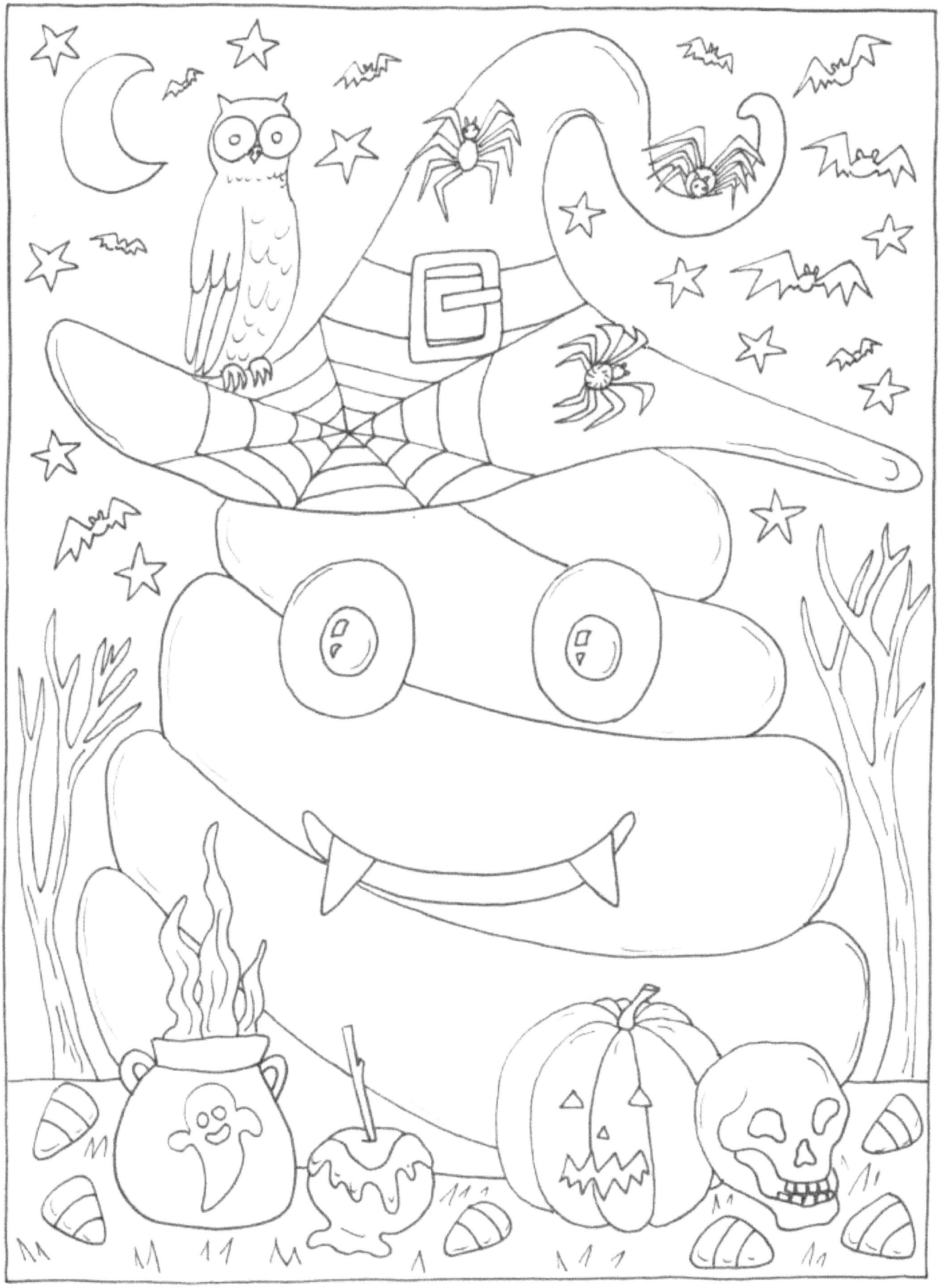

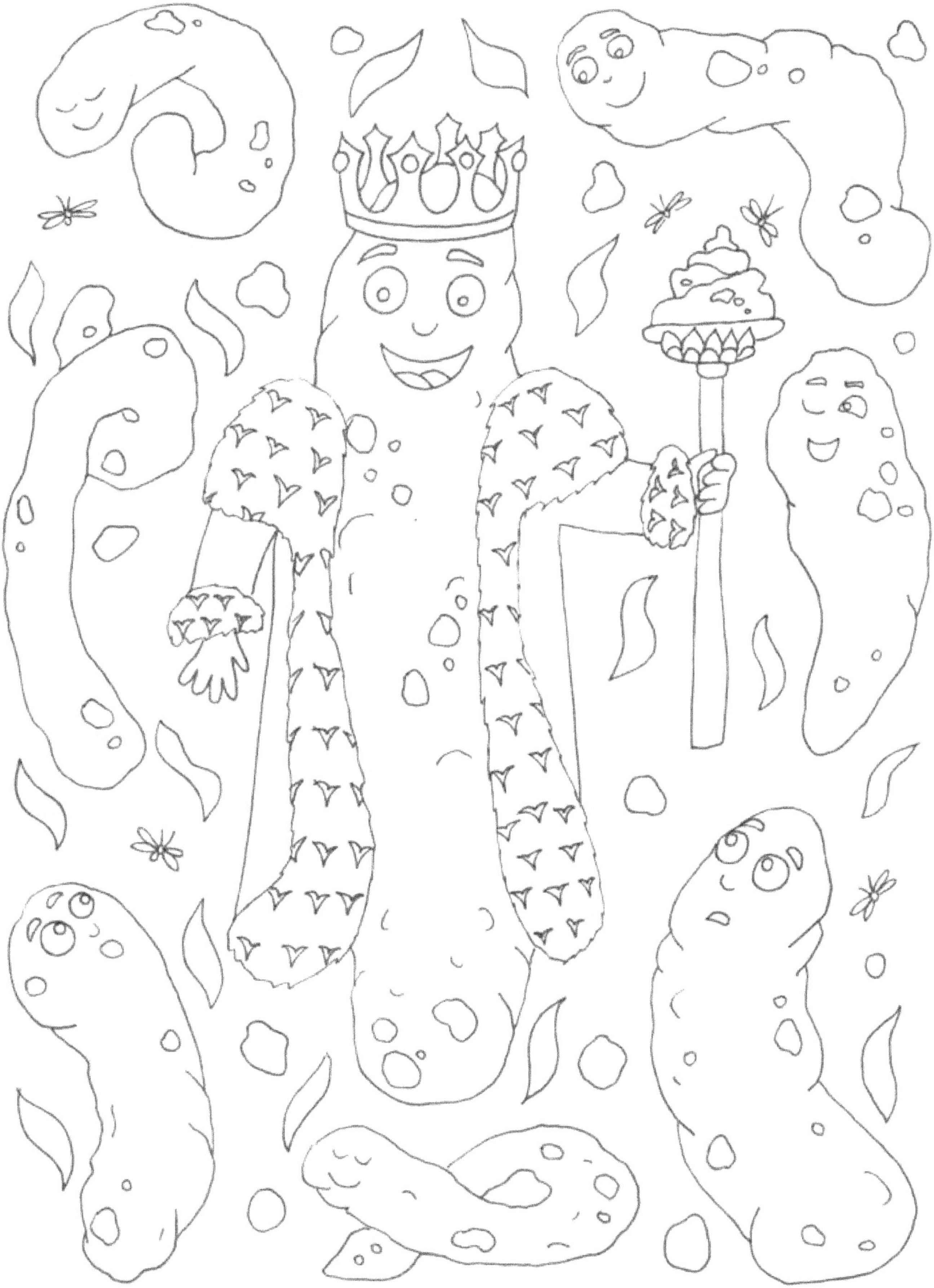

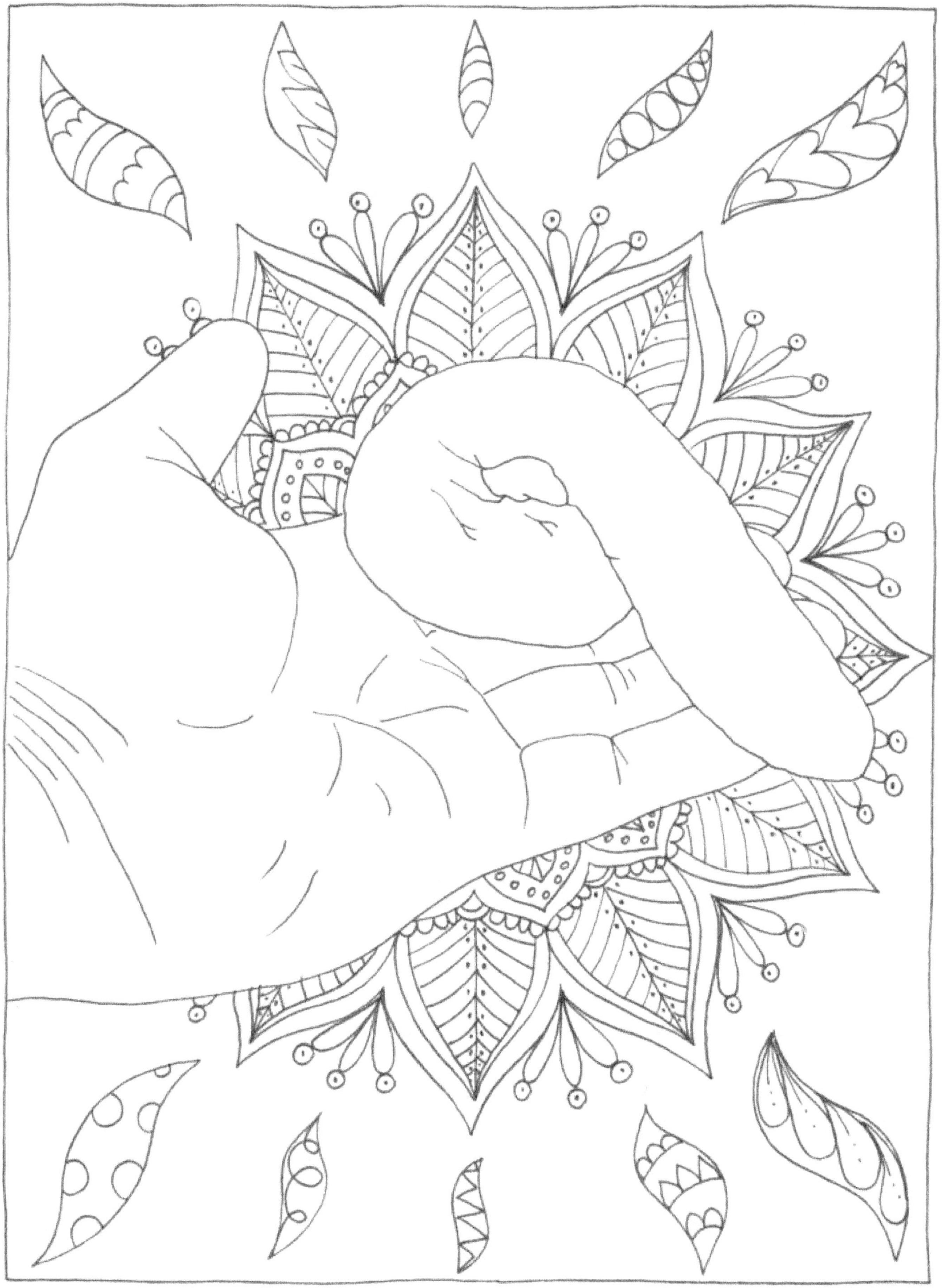

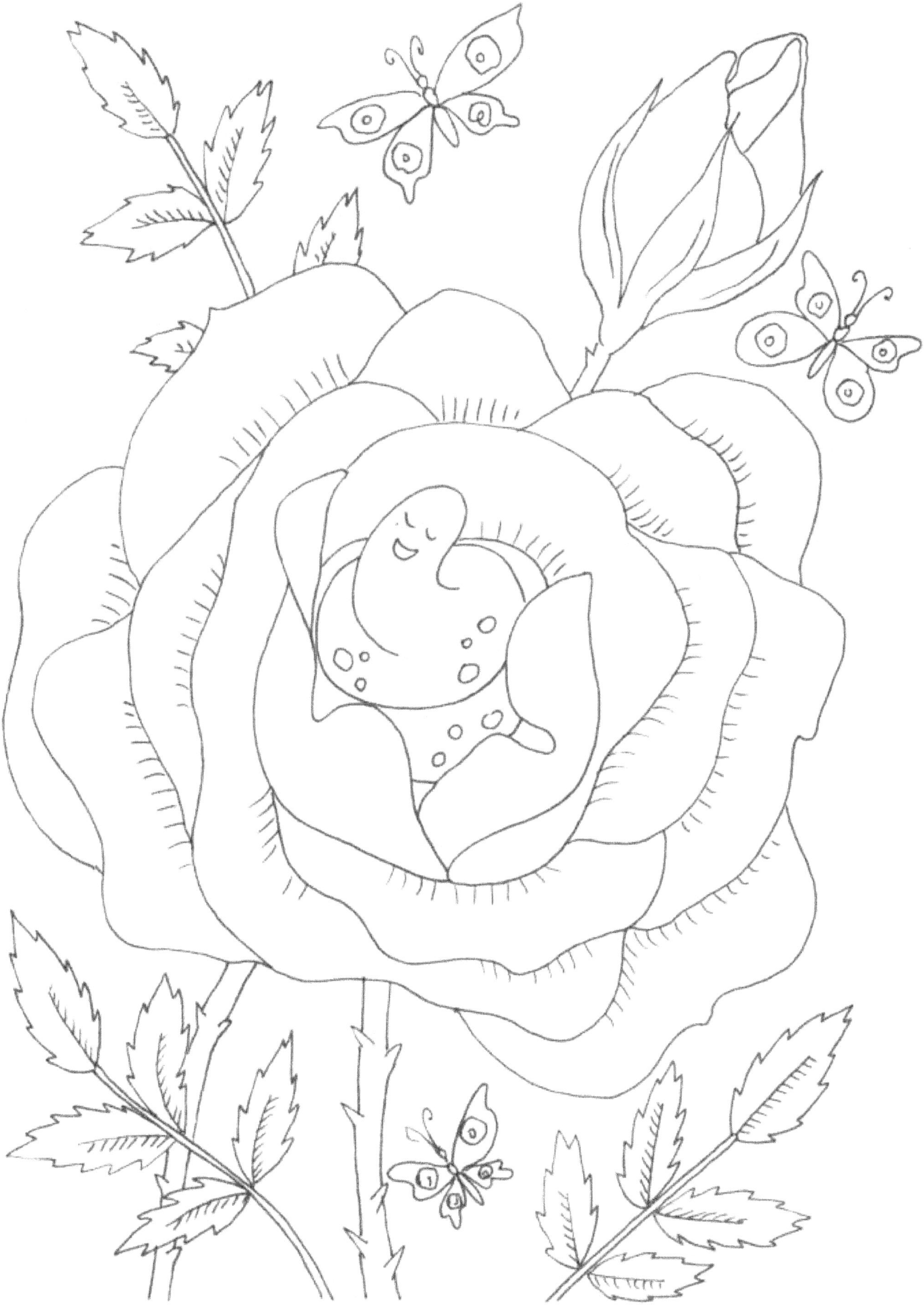

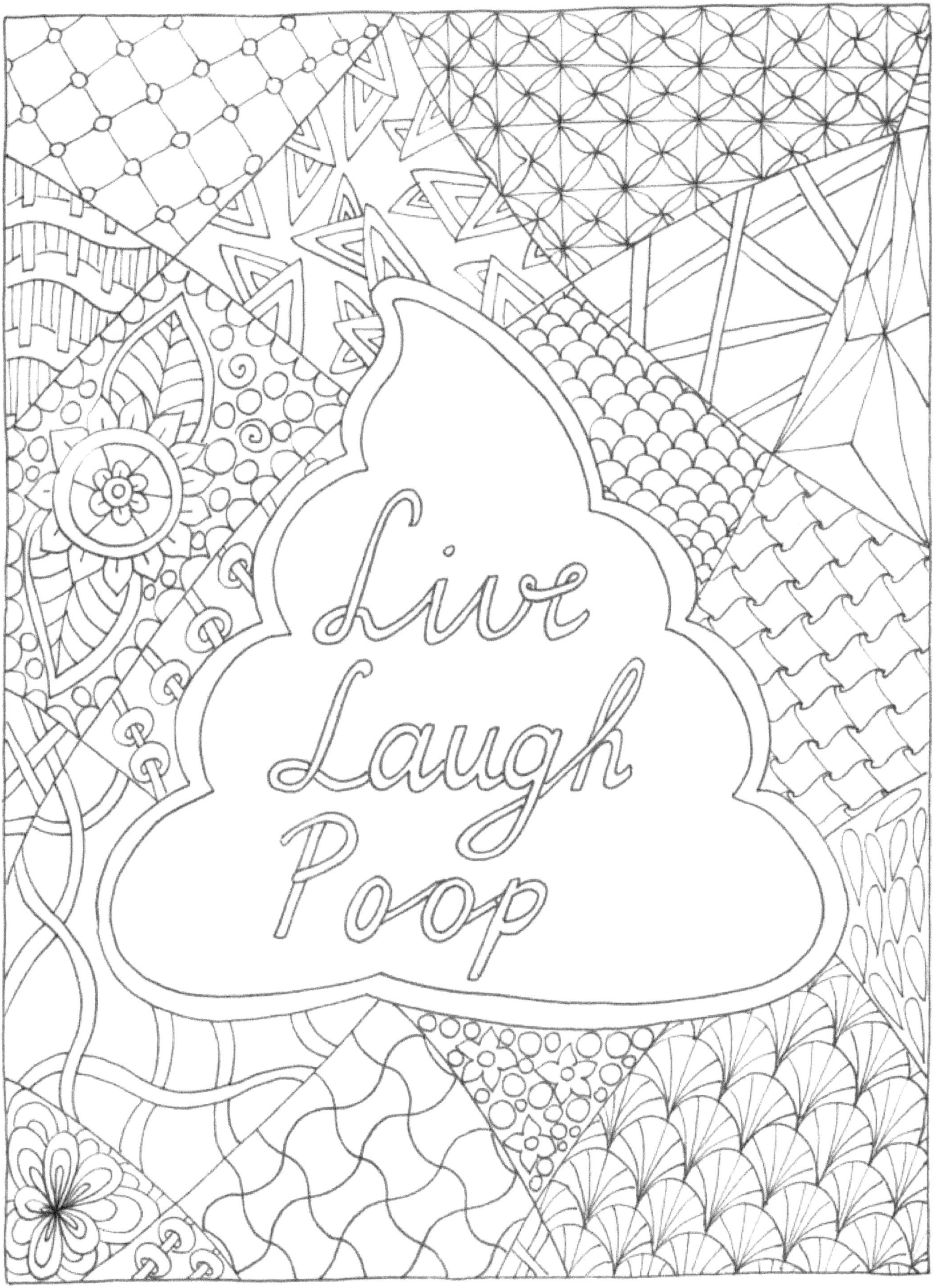
Live
Laugh
Poop

www.ingramcontent.com/pod-product-compliance
Lightning Source LLC
Chambersburg PA
CBHW062235220526
45471CB00009B/3495
* 9 7 8 1 9 8 6 0 3 1 5 4 7 *